Kit's Kip

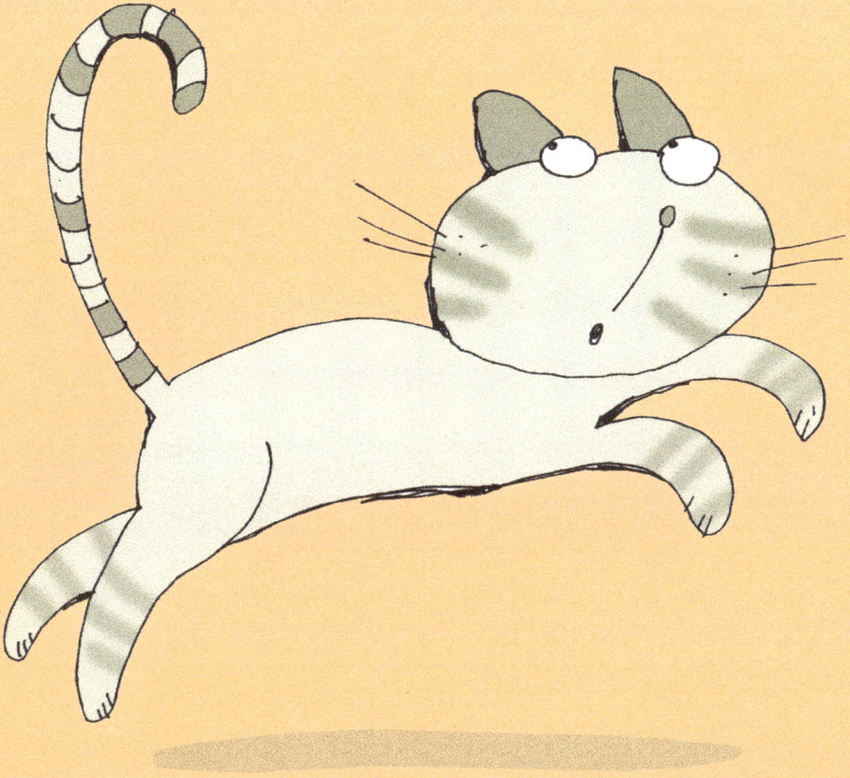

Written by Nicola Sandford
Illustrated by Jess Mikhail

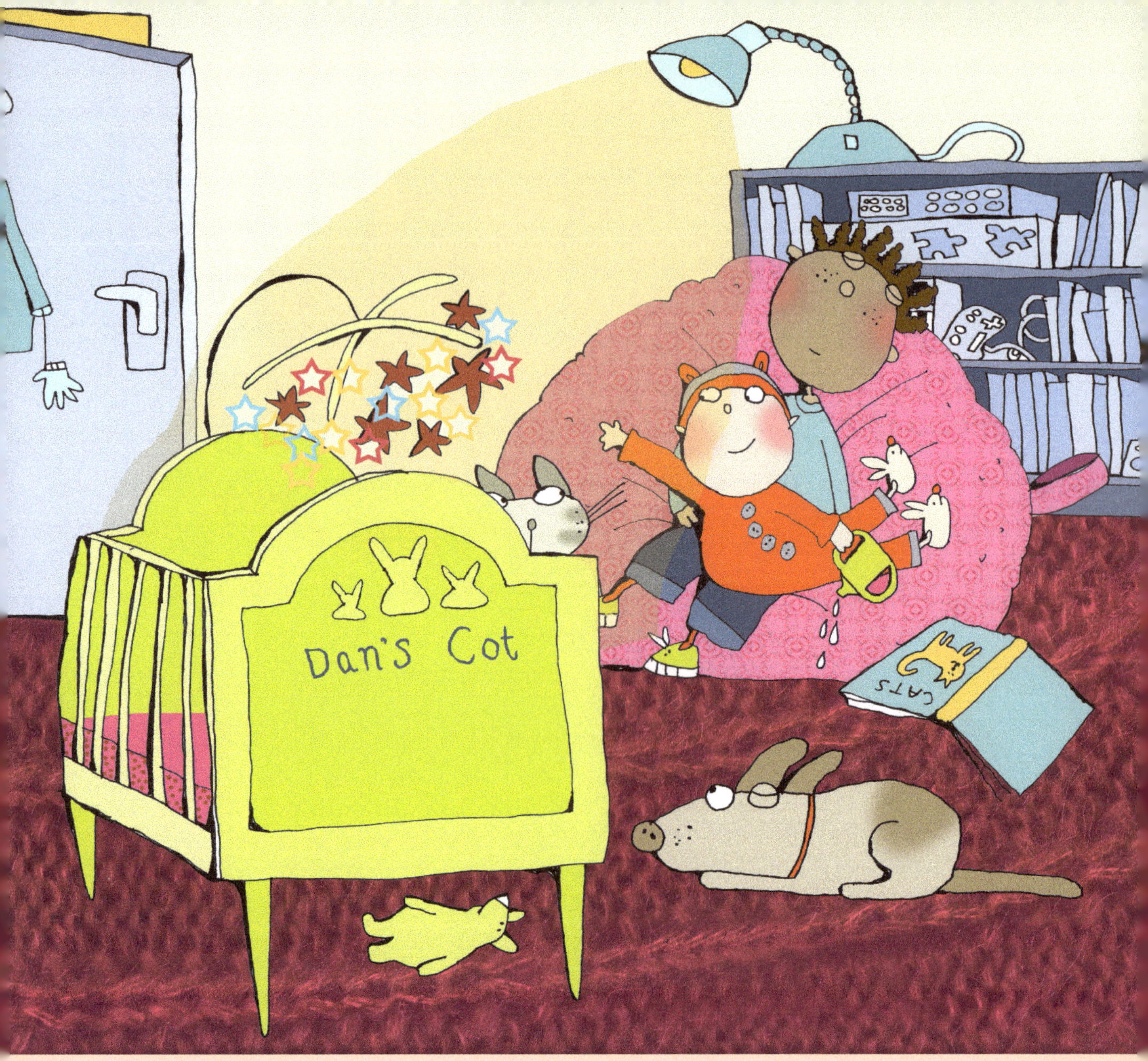

Kit is in Dan's cot.

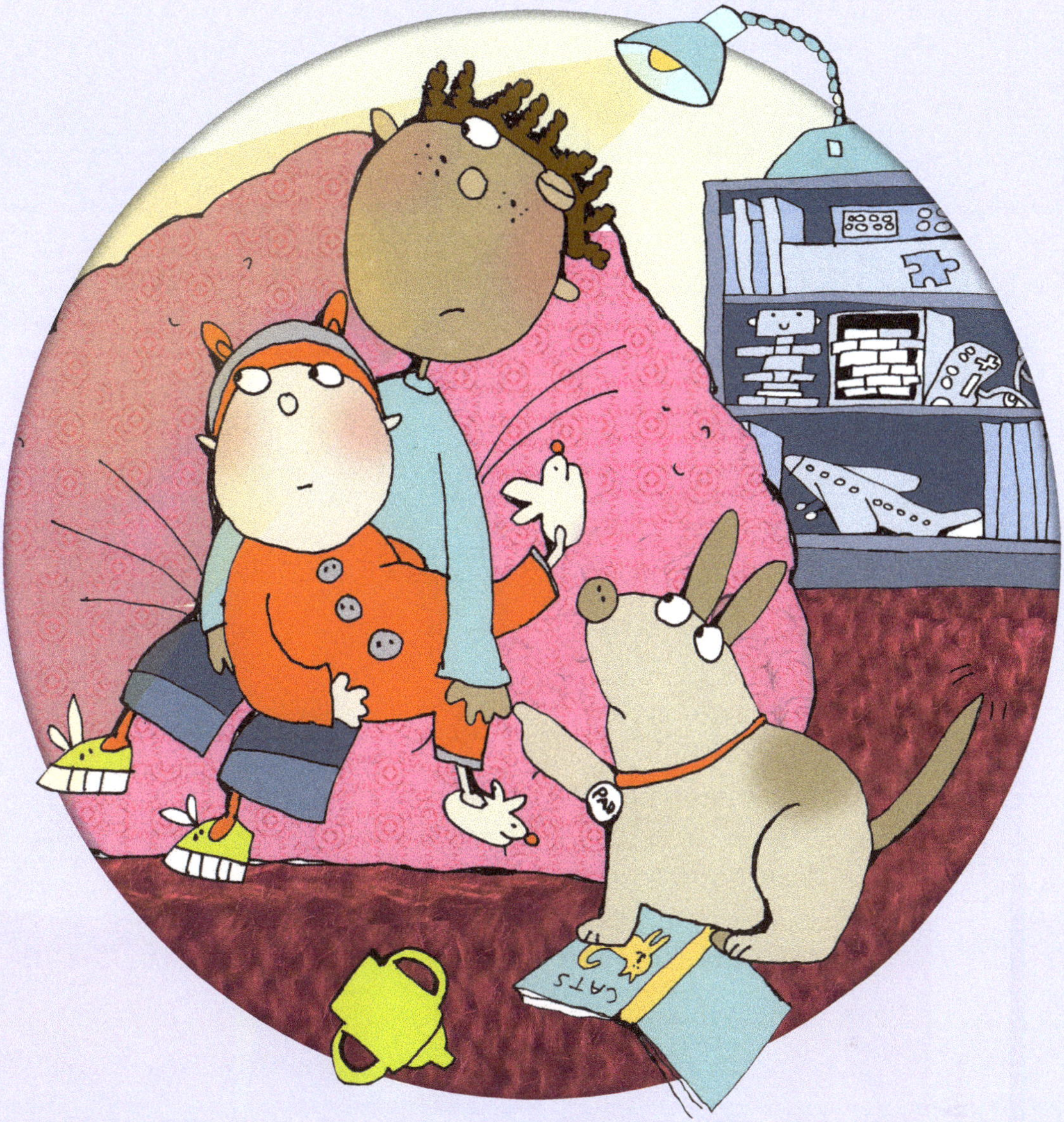

Pad taps Sid.

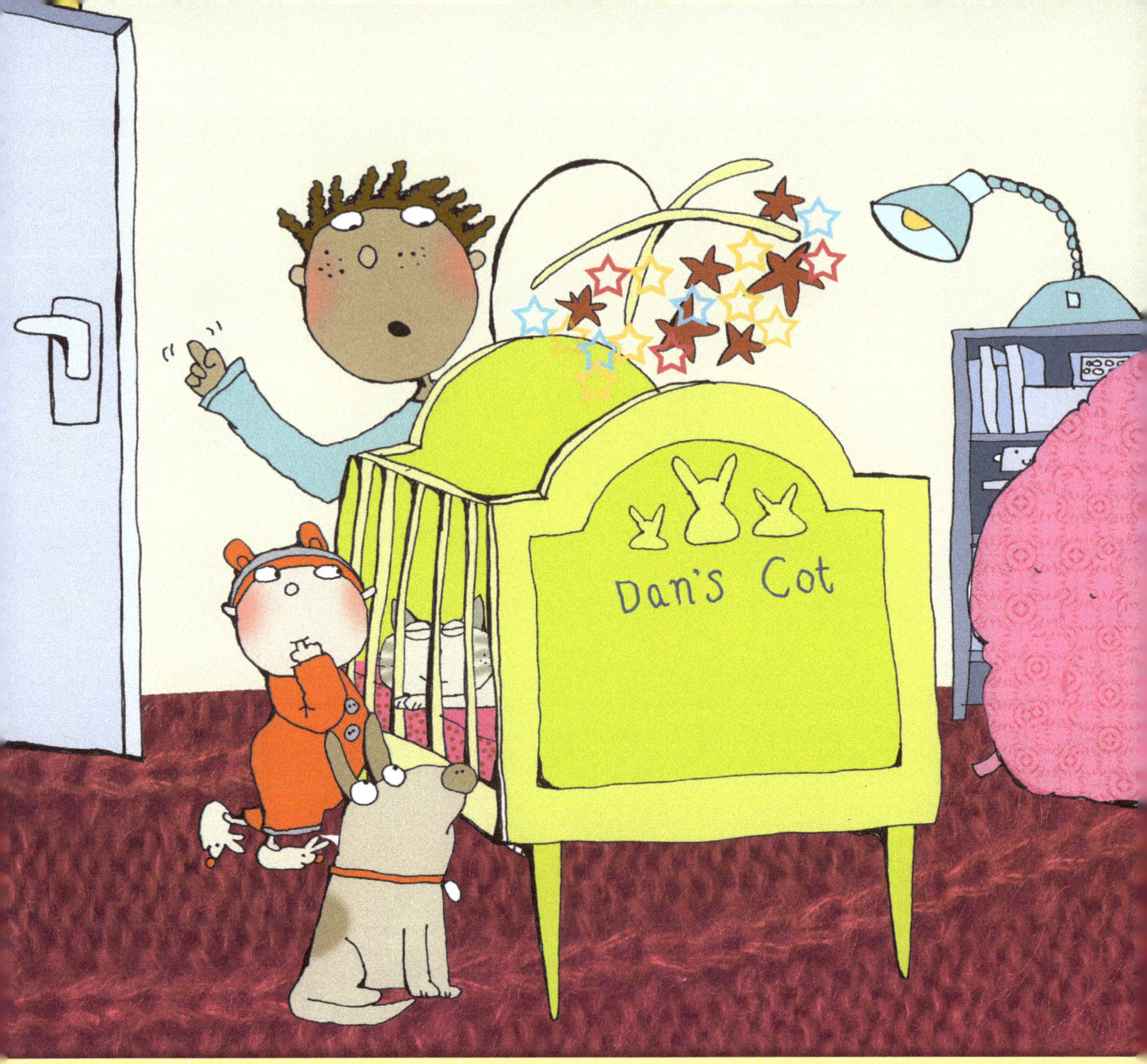

"Kit! Not in Dan's cot."

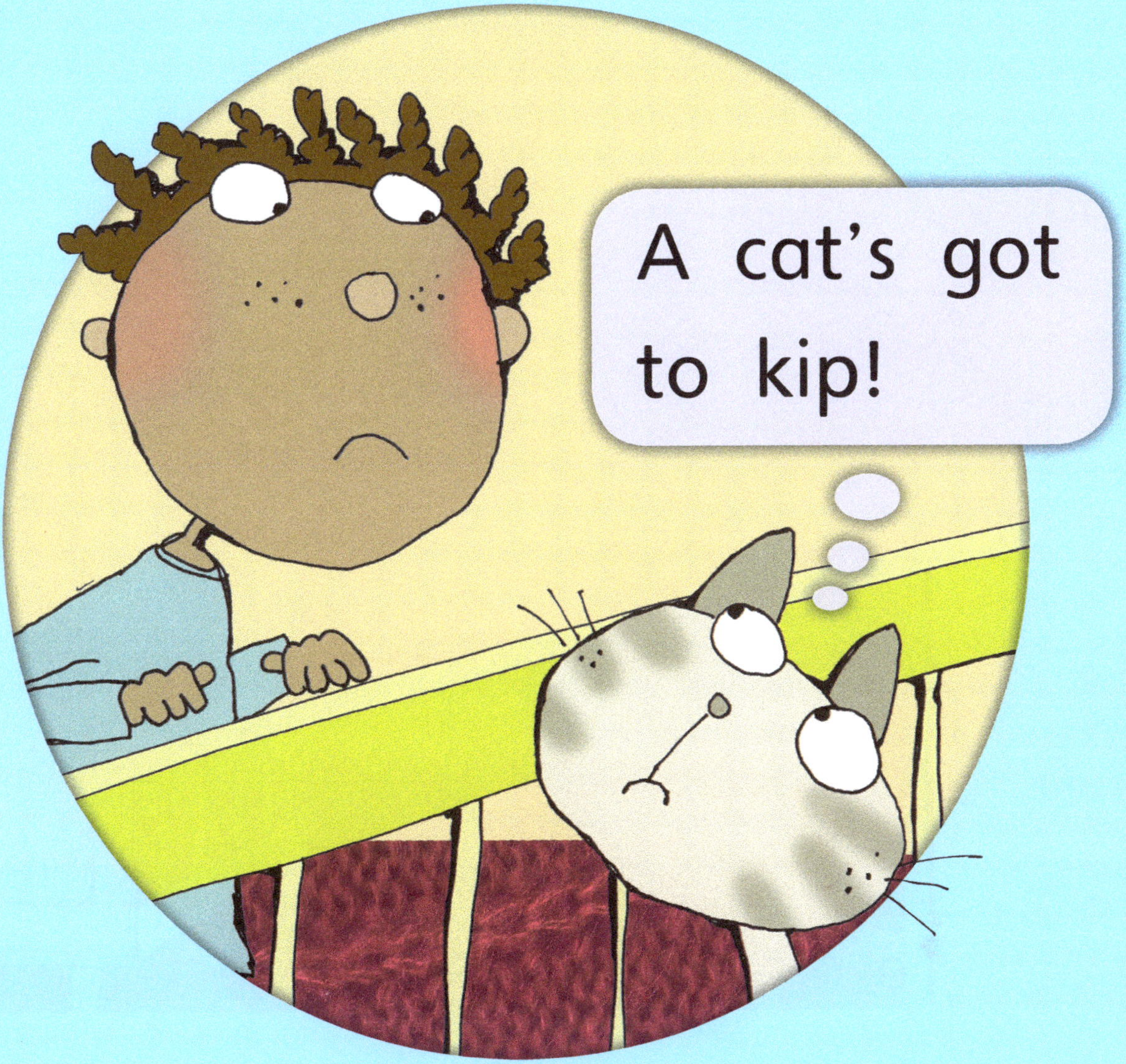
A cat's got to kip!

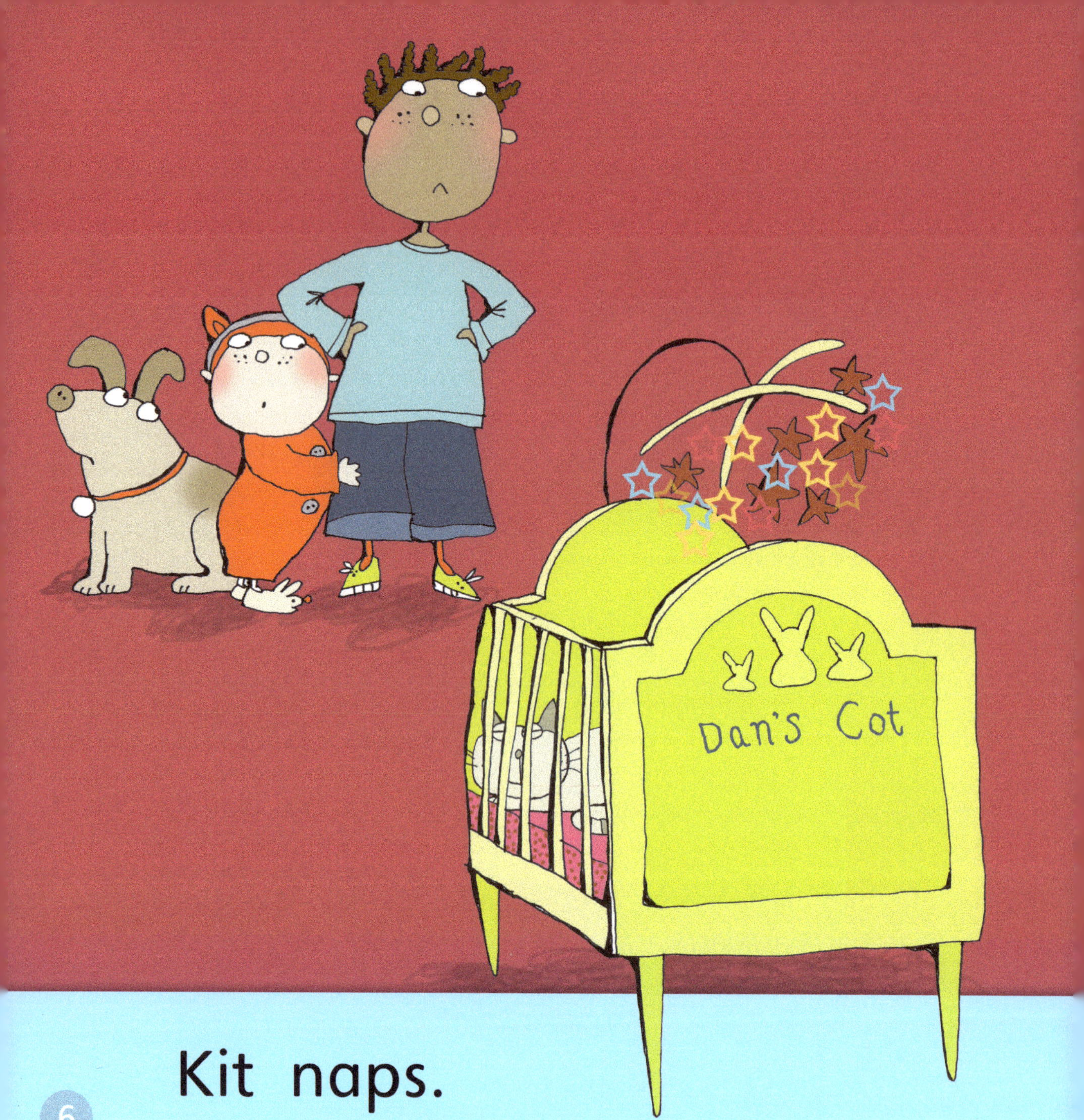

Kit naps.

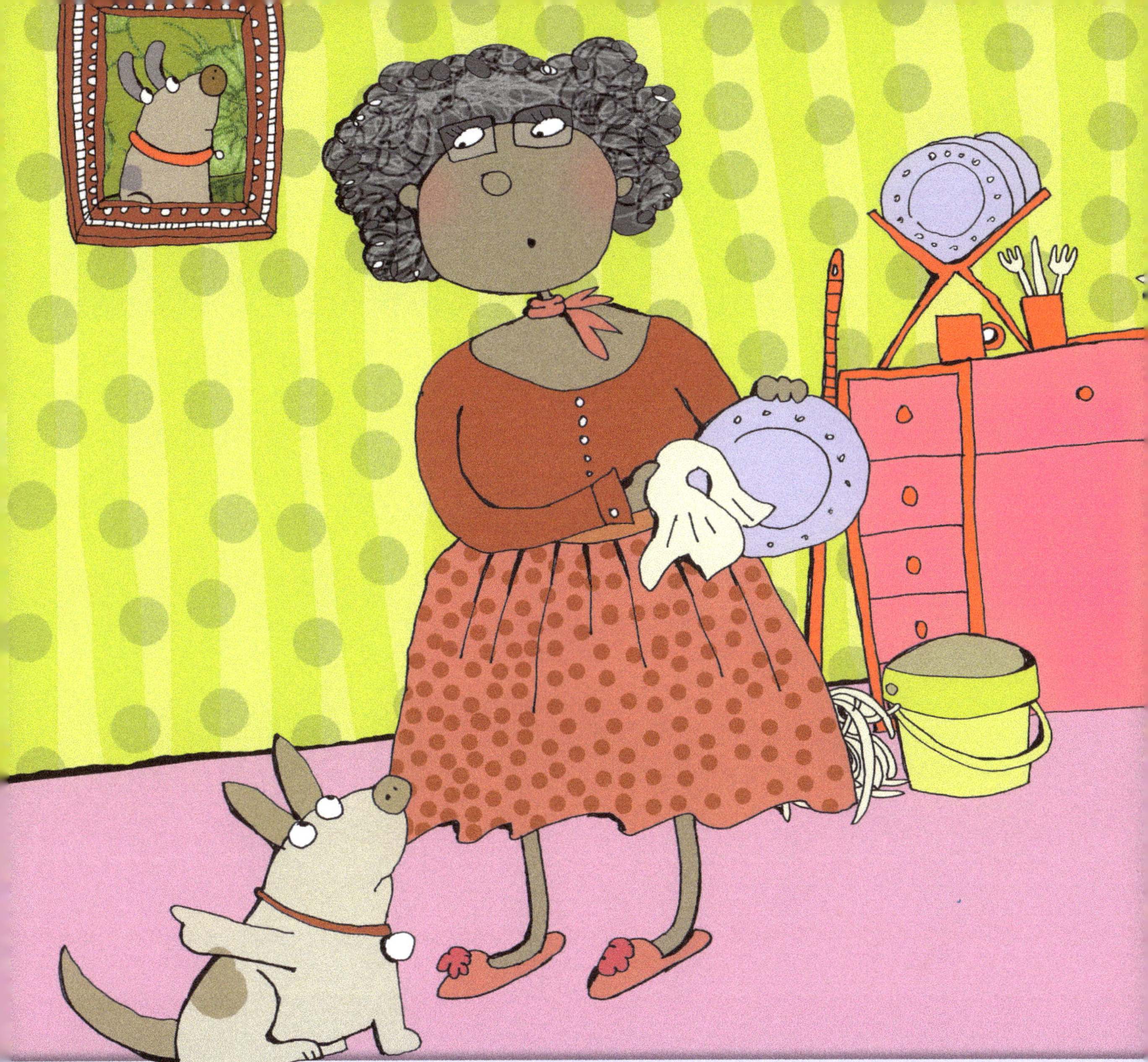

Pad got Nan.

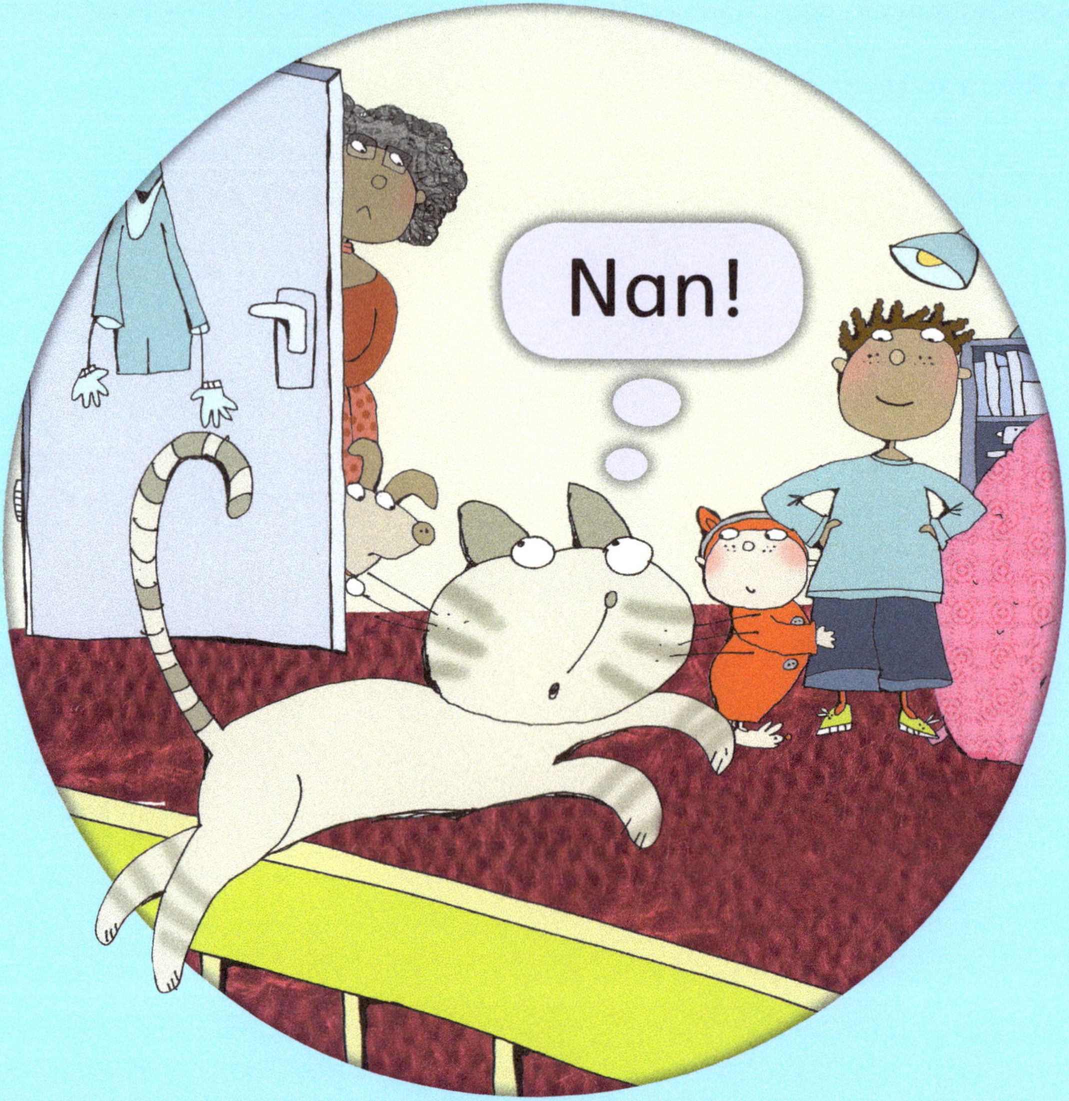

Kit is not in Dan's cot!